Family Hist

How to Trace your Ancestors

A Beginners Guide

Brian Smailes

Brian Smailes

Has been involved in family history for the past 10years and traced his ancestors back to the late 1500's. Brian is currently lecturing in family history in South Yorkshire at local colleges.

Due to the demands of the general public for more information on how to begin researching their family history, and the lack of information for people beginning their researches, Brian has produced this book to help the person 'in the street' discover their past.

With the aid of this easy to read book, he hopes you too will gain satisfaction in tracing your ancestors back to early times and producing your own family history file.

Family History, How to Trace Your Ancestors
First Published 2004
ISBN 1-903568-19-6
Challenge Publications
©

CONTENTS

Page

PLATES

INTRODUCTION

Family history is the fastest growing pastime in the country. Now you want to find your ancestors. Many resources are available to track down your long lost relatives, but how do you do it? Where do you go? What do you use? In this book I will attempt to explain how to get started and how to find, then record your findings so you have a lasting record of your hard work and no doubt many hours spent in research.

Resources are available in many forms, internet, libraries and archive departments, photographs, old maps, church records and printed certificates. How to find the best way to decipher these is what we need to know. I will attempt to show you this in the following pages.

Look on family history research as a piece of detective work. Take one step at a time, or on doing a jigsaw, put one piece in at a time before you move on to the next. The research and recording takes time, it is a marathon not a sprint but it can be rewarding. To find your ancestors going back to maybe 1500 or 1600 can be rewarding and self satisfying to know where you have descended from, to see how and where they lived and how they died.

Try to imagine what it would have been like for our ancestors back in 1700-1800, the clay pipes, candles on the table in dimly lit rooms, the open log fires but cold houses, food all home cooked and no cars, computers or televisions around. How did they travel, eat, work and live?

Come now to explore the world of yesterday and 'dig up' the past to reveal some no doubt startling discoveries on your family tree, and who knows perhaps a castle, knighthood or rich ancestor back in the realms of time. You may find a long lost branch of the family and even meet them after tracing the line back up through the generations as I have done.

Whatever your reasons for researching the past, I wish you luck in tracing your family tree!

WHAT YOU NEED

Before starting your research you will find it necessary to purchase the 'tools' you need for the job. These items are cheap and can be found readily available in many shops: -

During the gathering of information you will need to record it. To do this you need paper. I suggest A4 size sheets so you do not end up scribbling names etc on small pieces of paper that can get lost. Using A4 paper that is punched means you can then at least put them in a ring binder to both protect them and keep them in some kind of order.

Should you want to make a large size chart and put names on it as you find them then you should get either a roll of backing paper or a roll of wallpaper. You can then draw your chart on the reverse side and it can be as long as you want it.

When looking on the internet or visiting an archive resource centre you often have to work dates/ages out, either forwards from a census date or backwards, subtracting ages from census dates or similar. This all takes time so you will find it easier and quicker to have a pocket calculator that you can quickly put in the numbers and work out the ages. I find them a very useful, time saving and of course accurate tool.

When visiting an archive centre generally, you are not allowed to use a pen to record your findings as you can mark and damage the records. Use a pencil to record your information initially, writing it in pen at home only when you have confirmed your findings are correct. Pencils need sharpening so it is also worth getting a sharpener and a spare pencil as well as a rubber to correct mistakes.

Now you have a collection of paper, pencil, calculator etc, you need some clear plastic punched pockets that will fit into your ring binder to separate and protect your records.

Due to security reasons, you will find that in many of the research centres you are only allowed to take in the minimum of items, no bags, files, folders or other large items. You will find it easier if visiting, to just take one of these clear pockets with two or three sheets of A4 paper, pencils, calculator and any other small items that can be easily seen. The clear pockets are therefore the logical item to keep your records in when visiting a record office.

A ruler would be the final item on my list to help draw your tree or underline important notes. Now you have the 'tools', let's get started: -

HOW TO START

There is a wealth of information probably within living memory that your parents, grandparents, aunties and uncles have already. Begin by asking them the following: -

Names of relatives as far back as your relations can remember?
Dates of birth/death of relatives and ages of them when they died?
Maiden names of the females?
Areas where they were born or resided?
Jobs your relatives had?
Marriage dates and where they were married?
Military service?
Any old photographs?
Any birth/marriage/death certificates?
Any baptism certificates?
Is there a family bible with family details in it?

Any of the above information you can get, however little, will come in useful in helping you to trace your ancestors. You may not think some of it important but you will soon find all the above information very helpful in identifying the right people from the beginning then continuing through the generations.

As a beginner you need to be aware that if your name is Smith, Williams, Jones or any other popular name then it will be harder to find your relatives out of the thousands of these names, but not impossible. If you cannot find them one way then there is usually another avenue to go along.

Many people living pre1900 could not read or write, so names were spelt as the vicar, enumerator or registrar perceived how they should be spelt or how they heard them. Do not be surprised if you find your family surname is spelt differently back in 1800's and be prepared to search for slightly different spellings of your surname, if initially you cannot find details of relatives at a particular time.

Ask relatives if they have done any research themselves of the family names as this will save you time and effort in going over the same ground. Combine your results and involve other family members to help research individual lines of your tree.

When beginning family history you may find it easier to start by just tracing your direct male line back as far as you can. I say this because as a new starter, it is easier to trace the males, as usually the surname does not change so you are not looking for maiden names.

Along the way you will find other members of the family appearing in the records, which you can record to help build up a picture of the family. When you have the information, record it in generation order, then move on to the next generation so you do not get bogged down with one person or family unit.

The things you need to record if possible are: -

Marriage date and place of marriage
Date and place of birth
Date and place of death
Baptism date and place
Baptism certificate
Person married to, with their details
Photograph of church where married, baptised or buried if possible to put in your file
Photograph of the person or family for file
Copy of birth, marriage or death certificates for file (possible back to 1837)
Small map showing place of birth, to help make the file more complete

Photo No. 1

VISITING LOCAL STUDIES & ARCHIVE DEPARTMENTS

These departments hold a wealth of information. Initially you need to go and register and see just what information they have. Usually the information is free unless you visit a private record office where a small entry charge may be made.

On your first visit, explain to the reception staff that it is your first visit so they can show you where and how to use the facilities. Most of the local studies sections have the civil registration index, or what is commonly known as the St. Catherine's index. This is the national record of births, marriages and deaths, which have been in operation and use since 1837. Here you will probably find the first records of your ancestors. This index will be looked at in more detail in the next section.

Other records you may expect to find are parish records, census records generally from 1841 to 1901 (every ten years), registers of various religious denominations, electoral registers and copies of local newspapers often back into the 1850's as well as old maps and street plans of towns and villages. Every record office will have other records which are local to the area and which are valuable as a resource.

Remember when you visit to only take the items I listed in 'what you need' section and when you record the information to do it clearly and in some order. Once you are back at home, try to put the information in chronological order on your large main chart otherwise you will get bogged down with pieces of paper and information.

It is useful before you visit to have a number of names you want to research, so that if you come up against a barrier then you can look at the other names and dates you have and your visit will not be wasted. Generally you can at some point expect to come up against obstacles or not being able to find information on a particular person and things move slowly, then you get a breakthrough in your research and soon you are on track once again.

One thing you will find on your visits is that time will pass quickly while you are researching. A three-hour session passes very quickly and you may need longer or a return visit. It is a good idea to take a break during the day so you are still alert during your session and not missing any vital names or dates from your research due to fatigue.

CIVIL REGISTRATION (St. Catherine's Index)

Registration of births, deaths and marriages as we know it began on 1st July 1837. Any person who was born, married or died 'should' have been registered formally with the registration department. However, this did not always happen, and it was not until 1870 that the government made it compulsory for people to register all births etc. It is one of the most useful resources for tracing your family history.

Before 1929, marriages could take place between girls from twelve years old and boys from fourteen years old but this was changed in the Age of Marriage Act to sixteen years old for both boys and girls.

You may find no record of your ancestors when you look for them for a number of reasons: -

a. The person you are looking for was not registered, as sometimes happened. Some births were not registered at all so there is no official record, even though a marriage and death of that person may be recorded in later years. I have an ancestor who is recorded in marriage and on numerous census returns but his parents neglected to register his birth.

b. Some people did not register births until months after the event but said the baby had just been born when they registered it. This of course makes the child appear younger than they actually are.

c. Back in the 1700s – 1800s, many people could not read or write. Because of this, when they gave their names to the vicar for baptism, the enumerator for the census every ten years or to the registrar for births, deaths or marriage, it was left to that person how they heard or perceived the spelling of the name. The result was that people's surnames changed slightly. When you look in the records and cannot find a particular surname, try different ways of spelling it and you may have success.

In 1936, a Public Health Act was brought in, regarding registration of births. The doctor or nurse who attended the mother would inform the Medical Officer of Health of the birth and these details would be passed on to the registrar. This was a check to ensure that all births were registered within the time specified.

St.Catherine's Index can be read in many main libraries or archive departments as well as family history centres. You will find the records for the birth, death or marriage usually on microfiche and you use a 'viewer' or 'reader' there to read it.

Although the early years are handwritten, with some hard to read and some illegible, the majority are readable, with the later ones typed. The fiches are in alphabetical order and when placed individually in the fiche reader, the following information is shown: -

1. The birth, death or marriage month is placed in quarters, e.g. March, June, September or December.
2. A reference number is given.
3. The name of the town where the birth etc was registered is shown.
4. The full name of the person registered is shown.
5. The age of the person (on the death index).

First identify your ancestor in the index then send for a copy of the original certificate. This will ensure that you obtain official confirmation of your ancestors existence.

Before you send for the certificate however, look at a census or parish record to link and cross reference as a double check to ensure you have the right ancestor and that you are not finding a complete strangers ancestors by mistake. It is easy to go off on the wrong track when you are starting your research so always check. It can also prove expensive sending for certificates by mistake for people who are no relation.

You should apply to the register office that is shown on the index for a copy of the certificate, not to your local register office. The other place you can apply to is Southport (address in back of book), but there the certificates currently cost between £8.00 to over £30.00 depending how much information you can give them, and if they have to do a search to find it. In general register offices the certificates cost £7.00 in 2003.

Some register offices will process your request and send the certificates by return of post; others take weeks to deal with your request. It is worth telephoning the office first to check payment details and address, and if they have the certificate you require.

To obtain addresses of the various register offices around the country, contact your local archives, library or register office who usually have all the addresses or look on the internet at the Genuki website, (see useful websites).

READING THE INFORMATION

Certificates are the best way of proving your relations existed, as well as a link back to the previous generation or forward to the next. Obtaining the certificate then checking the information carefully is important.

A **birth certificate** will show the following main details: -

When & Where Born	First Name	Sex	Name & Surname of Father	Name, Surname & Maiden Name of Mother	Fathers Occupation	Signature, Description & Residence of informant

If you do purchase a certificate and it states 'the mark of' in the signature column, this usually indicates the person who registered the birth could not write so they put X as their mark. Many people signed like this and this is how names were often changed slightly, as the registrar wrote it how he thought it should be written.

This gives you a link back to the previous generation by showing the names of the parents and importantly the mother's maiden name so you can then look for her birth details. Usually if you work back twenty to twenty-five years then you can find the parents birth, unless of course it was a large family and the parent could have been in her late thirties or even forties by the time she stopped having children.

The place of birth was often the home where the parents were living. Other details like father's occupation and child's full name help you to piece together details of the family and to build up a more complete picture. This information can be cross-referenced with a census return, which it is important to do, and it will ensure you are recording the right family and have not ventured to another family by mistake.

Go back approximately one to ten years depending if the child is the first-born or the last and you may find the marriage in the registers, of the parents.

The **marriage certificate** will give the following information: -

Date of Marriage	Name & Surname (of both people)	Ages	Condition eg.Spinster	Profession	Residence at time of Marriage	Fathers Name & Surname	Profession

The date and place of marriage was usually the place where the bride lived at the time. The ages shown on the certificate help you confirm known dates of birth and approximate ages of parents. The residence on the certificate shows where the people were residing at the date of marriage. The other valuable piece of information is the father's name and occupation. This establishes the link with the past, joining the generations together.

The Hardwicke Marriage Act came into force in 1754 and this ensured that banns were called before all marriages took place unless they were by licence. It also ensured that all marriages took place in the Parish Church apart from Jews or Quakers.

On the top of the marriage certificate it states whether the marriage is by banns, licence or certificate. If the marriage were by licence, there would have to be a Marriage Bond/Allegation. These were quite expensive at the time, but gave details such as the man's occupation, where he lived and his age. Libraries or archives in the areas your ancestors lived may hold bound copies of these covering different years.

Below are shown the details required on a Marriage Bond Allegation in 1819

Date of Marriage Bond/Allegation _____

Bondsmen x 2
Name _____ **Signature**_____
Residence_____
Occupation_____

Male Party
Name _____
Residence_____
Occupation _____
Age _____
Status - eg Batchelor

Female Party = Same as above

Marriage to take place in eg.Holy Trinity **Church, Place** eg. Leeds

You may be able to view Marriage Bond/Allegations in your local archives or write to The Borthwick Institute, York for a copy if you are certain your ancestors were married in this way. (Address in Wills section).

At the bottom of the marriage certificate it will show the signatures of the bride and groom. This will have written 'the mark of' if they cannot write.

Witnesses' names on a marriage certificate may well be relations of the bride or groom or could be only friends. It was not uncommon, particularly in the first half of the 1800's for the witnesses as well as the bride and groom to be unable to read or write and for all four people to mark with an X on the register, hence they were known as 'marksmen'.

Looking forward approximately forty to fifty years you may be able to find the death in St. Catherine's register of the parent.

The **death certificate** will show: -

When & Where Died	Name & Surname	Sex	Age	Occupation	Cause of Death	Signature, Description & Residence of Informant	When Registered

The place of death is often the place of residence. It also gives you the occupation of the deceased at death. This will help you to cross reference with other existing information to ensure you are tracing the right person. Look carefully at the details of the informant as it is often a son, daughter, or other relation and together with their address helps you to find out more about them. The details at the top of the death certificate show the place where the death was registered.

Again, all these details help to link people dates and places together to form a family tree. When working out dates forward and backwards from ages on the certificates, you will find a calculator a valuable tool.

Once you have obtained the death certificate, you may also find it helpful to see if there are any newspapers in existence for that time. Look in the newspapers of the time, around a week after the death, and you may find the announcement of the death. It may give the names of the relations of the deceased, which will help your research. Try to get a copy of the announcement for your records.

As a footnote to the information on deaths etc, you may be interested to know that in 1667 and 1678, Acts of Parliament were passed, known as the Acts of Burial in Woollen. This was a move designed to stimulate the trade in wool and sheep farming although it was the king having the idea there was a captive market for shrouds.

The law stated that a person must be buried in a woollen shroud, unless they had died from the plague. In some parish records it states that a person had been buried 'according to the law'. There was a £5.00 fine if the law was not upheld. This law was not repealed until 1814.

In 1694 there was a sliding scale of registration fees for burials, marriages and baptisms, the high fees payable if you had a title. At the other end of the scale, there was no tax payable if you were a pauper, so you may well find the parson writing the letter 'P' in the parish register beside the entry so a parishioner would not have to pay the tax. So all the people with a 'P' against their name in a parish register were not necessarily paupers.

People who committed suicide were buried without a religious ceremony. They were usually buried at a crossroads (so their spirit would not know which way to go) with a stake through their heart!

Any ancestors who may have been hung, were usually buried within the grounds of the prison they were hung in, although some prisoners in the seventeen and eighteen centuries were hung in chains at the crossroads out of the City.

Photo No. 2

CENSUS RETURNS

These were started in limited form in 1801 then every ten years thereafter to the present time (apart from 1941). The next census release is in 2011 due to the 100-year rule. Generally you can view copies of census returns dating back to 1841. Some people did not appear on a census for a variety of reasons and to this day some still do not want to, and simply disappear on census day. Occasionally you may find this with some of your past ancestors.

Another reason for not finding people on a census is that a name may be spelt differently to what you think so you are looking for the wrong name. Again as with birth certificates, when the enumerator knocked on the house door on census day back in 1861, he would probably have to fill in the census form himself so how he heard a name was how he probably wrote it. If you could not find a relative in a census, that you know should be there, try looking for similar sounding names or slightly different spellings.

A census return gives an insight into the make up of a family. Although the early census returns did not give all the information we now expect from a census, those from 1851 onwards improved, and a lot of valuable information can be gained. A census will (on most census returns) give the following information: -

Address	Name/Surname	Relation To Head of Family	Condition eg. Married	Age	Rank, Profession or Occupation	Where Born	Deaf/ Dumb/ Blind

You can find a complete family, parents, children, often a lodger, with their ages and employment. Many houses had a lodger living with them; especially in the late 1800s and into the 1930s. Viewing a census return is like opening the door of a house and seeing all the family gathered there

Sometimes on census returns, if you look at nearby houses you may see another relation living close by. I have found in my researches, parents and siblings living in the same street.

It is important to look closely at census returns as these do link generations. Once you have the information it will help you to go back to the next generation if you work out the dates of birth of the parents or grandparents shown then look in the parish records or in St. Catherine's index to find their birth or death.

To work out ages of people, it is important to know the census dates, these were:-
4/6/1841   30/3/1851   7/4/1861   2/4/1871   3/4/1881   5/4/1891   31/3/1901

OBTAINING INTERNET INFORMATION

The computer is a modern day tool to aid genealogists and the internet is even more valuable. There is a wealth of information that can be obtained from the internet. Census returns for 1881 and 1901, birth, marriage and death details and military lists, even records of people who were deported to Australia as prisoners can be found.

To get the best from the internet you need to be fully conversant with its use and how to access the many web sites for information. If you can do this it will greatly assist you in your researches. A short list of some of the best web sites are shown in 'useful research contacts' in the back of this book.

Many of the sites are free or partially free but to access some information you have to subscribe. Generally the majority of people can often find the information they want from free sources, paying only for copies of birth, marriage or death certificates, once you have found the right information.

There is a wealth of information contained on CD's for use on a home computer that can be purchased to help your research. Many family history societies and private companies produce CD's, microfiche and other data and these are available from the individual family history societies who have the data for their own areas. Private companies who specialise in CD's usually advertise in family history magazines that are on sale in the high street.

Through the private companies you are able to purchase items like the complete 1891 census for a county on a set of CD's or a marriage index for a County. There is a wide variety of CD's and Microfiche for sale, so it may be worth buying a family history magazine from your local newsagents to see what is on offer. Census returns and other statistical information can be printed from your printer and can then be inserted into your file you are compiling.

PARISH RECORDS

These often date back to the early 1500's for many churches and can usually be found in the local studies, libraries or archive department. Thomas Cromwell was the man who ordered every baptism, marriage or burial to be recorded. Going back in time, you can research St. Catherine's index back to 1837 as well as church records, then only church records from 1837 back to around 1538 or earlier if you can get them. Many of the records are now on reels of film; some are typed in transcript form in books, which are easy to read.

The records available are generally baptism, marriage and burial records. Some records may be missing due to neglect and/or bad storage by the church they were kept in, often having been stored in damp conditions in a vault or other room between the 1600s – 1900s. All records now are looked after more carefully to preserve history for future generations.

In previous centuries there were quite a lot of illegitimate children born. Illegitimacy crops up in most families at one time or another. These were still recorded in the church records as most people, married or not, still had their babies baptized. It was often common practice in the 1850s to have baptisms on Christmas Day and weddings too. You may find your relation was baptised on Christmas Day.

In early parish records the name of the child baptized was given and the name of the father but not always the name of the mother. This shortage of information will not help your research.

Before 1754, baptism, marriage and burial records were often written together on the same pages in church registers. This all changed however in 1754 when registers were introduced with separate columns and set questions to be answered and blank boxes to be completed. This went a long way in improving the record keeping of the church. The same system is still in operation to the present day.

Many records for 1500-1600 were written in Latin, but with the aid of a Latin dictionary, these can be explained. They provide interesting reading of the names of people at that time.

Church records were often copied and these were known as the Bishops' Transcripts. These records have been kept since 1597, then an Act of 1598 ordered that each year a copy of all the past years registers should be sent to the bishop. Many of these transcripts are held at archive offices but some are still with the bishops at the Cathedrals. Should you find the parish record missing or illegible, look for the bishops' transcripts, which may hold the missing information.

WILLS

Through the centuries many people have left Wills. The last 'Will and Testament' literally meant their property and their possessions, and these details were duly written so that when they died their property; land and possessions could be passed on to their successors.

Most people were allowed to make Wills, from the age of twelve for a boy and fourteen for a girl. A married woman could not make a will without her husbands consent unless she was married after 1882 when the Married Women's Property Act applied.

Before 1858, the country was split into two sections, north and south. South came under the Prerogative Court of Canterbury while the north came under the court of York. York records are held at Borthwick Institute of Historical Research, St. Anthony's Hall, Peasholme Green, York YO1 2PW Tel 01904 642315 and date from 1388 to 1858.

Details of Wills in the south of the country 1383-1858 are on microfilm and copies can be seen at the Public Records Office or The Family Records Centre.

All Wills proved after January 1858 can be inspected (charge made) at The Probate Search Room, The Probate Service, Principal Registry of the Family Division, First Avenue House, 42 – 49 High Holborn, London WC1V 6NP. If you know the date of death, photocopies of wills can be ordered (charge made) from The Court Service, York Probate Sub-Registry, Duncombe Place, York YO1 2EA Tel. 01904 671564.

Wills can give a lot of information about families, wealth, possessions, and how your ancestors lived, worked and died right back to early times. It is perhaps a branch of genealogy you may want to explore once you are well underway with your family tree and file. It will provide a new dimension to your family history file.

There are many other aspects to Wills and other avenues to explore in this complicated legal field, so the above is only intended as an introduction to show that information is available should you wish to search for it.

If you are unsure if your ancestors left a Will, look to see if they owned a house or a piece of land. If they did then they will probably have made a Will. Many archive departments hold bound copies of lists of people who made Wills with the dates. You then have to apply as described above for a copy of the Will.

COLLECTING PHOTOGRAPHS

Since around 1840 when photography was first invented, photographs have been taken of people, places and even from outer space. Photographs are important to genealogists as they provide a link with their ancestors and the past. Not only can we look at the photographs of our ancestors as a lasting reminder but also of the houses they lived in and areas they grew up in.

Photographs can tell us more than we think at first sight. Take the photograph of a wedding (Photo 1). This photo, although not too old, shows the following: -

- a. The Wedding family.
- b. Look at the wide lapels on the men's jackets.
- c. The style of the bridesmaids dresses.
- d. The style of hat the man on the right is wearing.
- e. The size of the bunches of flowers the bridesmaids are holding.
- f. The colour and type of photograph for dating it.

Even if you do not know the date of a photograph, by making enquiries, you can usually date a picture, in this case 1928, by the style of clothing worn or another feature on it particular to that moment in time it was taken.

Old photographs, which you see in books, of houses and streets, show us just what it was like to live in the towns and villages back in the 1800's and the turn of the last century. That is why it is so important to not only collect names for a family tree but to assemble a photographic collection of people and the streets and houses where they existed as a visual reminder of where they lived and of their lives.

Any photographs you can get of relations and the area they lived in should be carefully kept and inserted into your file. Make sure you put names of people on the back so others know who they are. Photographs that have been damaged can be restored. There are specialist shops that can do repairs but these days many people can restore photographs on their home computer. Ensure any damaged photo's are repaired and copied so you have a lasting record of long lost ancestors.

The photograph in (Photo 2) has been restored and is the only photograph in existence of these three people. When found, this photograph was torn and only 8cm by 5cm in size. Note the flat caps they are wearing and the bowler hat belonging to the front person, also the wide lapels of the jackets along with the style of the shirt collars. This photograph was taken in 1937.

CHURCHYARD EXPLORATION

When doing your research, you may find the name of a church where your ancestor was buried. I strongly recommend visiting the church to look at the headstones in the churchyard. Headstones will often tell you the date of birth and death, and how old the person was. They may have the name of the husband or wife on also, and if you are lucky it may be a family plot with other ancestors names on.

You may not find a headstone, but all is not lost because if you can look inside the church, you may find a plaque on a wall, name or other inscription carved on a pew/or pulpit or even a window in the church with your ancestors name on it. This very much depended on how important the person was in the local community or whether they were a churchwarden at that church, or other prominent person, maybe the parson himself.

When visiting a church, have a good look and take a camera for photographs of headstones or of the church itself, as this may be the only record of a person being baptised, married or buried there and it is important to put the details or photograph in your family history file.

Looking at headstones, you may find it helpful to take a stiff hand brush or even a wire brush, as many headstones are covered with lichen and other vegetation and it may be difficult to read the inscription on them until you have given them a brush. As for the very old and obliterated headstones, take some paper and a wax crayon to do a rubbing of the headstone if necessary if this is the only way of obtaining the information on the stone.

If a headstone is found in a parish churchyard, check for a will. I have found that one often goes with the other. Not many people could afford a headstone, but if they did, they may have had money, which meant they might also have left a will.

In some churchyards the headstones have all been removed. If this has happened, the vicar at the church may have a plan of the burial site and a list of names of those buried. The local archive department or the Council department responsible for looking after cemeteries may have the information if the vicar does not.

Some churches or even the local family history society may have documented the inscriptions on all the gravestones in the churchyard, so it is worth finding out if a list exists for your particular churchyard.

Finally as far as the church is concerned, when you visit, if there are any small booklets available about the church and its history, buy one to put in your file. It will make good reading in ninety years time for your great grandchildren.

OTHER USEFUL INFORMATION

When children were born, it was a common practice back in the 1800s to name children after relations. This is still done today although not as often and not in the same order as then. The format generally followed was: -

1st son after the fathers father	1st daughter after the mother's mother
2nd son after the mothers father	2nd daughter after the father's mother
3rd son after the father	3rd daughter after the mother

Not everyone followed this pattern, but it may help you when searching for names to perhaps pay more attention to names that keep re-occurring in parish registers or in the St. Catherine's Index.

Between 1696 and 1822 there was a tax on every house known as the 'window tax'. This was charged throughout the country and records for this are often held in local archive offices. These records will help to establish where a person was living at a particular time. You may see old buildings with some windows bricked up and this was done to avoid paying the window tax.

There are many records available, particularly on the internet of convicts, prisoners, hangings in various prisons like York and Durham and of deportations to Australia, as well as people executed for witchcraft. This may seem at first irrelevant to your family tree, but do not ignore it completely. All those prisoners were someone's relations, and they may be yours when you get back to that particular time in history, keep an open mind.

There is a wealth of information on the internet of military campaigns, militia muster records from 1757. You can also find records of people who fought in other wars like the Boer War, the Battle of Waterloo and the Crimea War. The information available gives names of soldiers/sailors, and there are records of commendations and medals awarded. The Commonwealth War Graves Commission has an excellent website covering military personnel who died in the first and second world wars. Should you think that your ancestors at some point fought for king and country, then check out the web sites. Much of the information I have found is on the Genuki website at www.genuki.org.uk

In many archives around the country, poor law records are held. These are records from the parishes of people who were supported by the parish. Some people, like now, fell on hard times and were given assistance, some worked in the workhouse. These poor law and workhouse records can be found in many local archives.

Throughout the centuries, many religions have been born. John Wesley's Methodist movement started back in 1757 then branched into numerous sections. Others like the Quakers, Roman Catholics, Presbyterians, United Reform, Baptists, Congregationalists and many others all flourished at times, now some have all but disappeared. These groups were called non-conformists.

As well as the general parish records which I have already mentioned most of these church groups kept records of their congregations, churchwardens and officers as well as their own birth, marriage and death records. Many of these can be found today in local archives throughout the country. Again, if you think your ancestor was a member of one of these religions then check the records.

When compiling your family history file, you may like to put in some maps of the area where you know your ancestors lived. If there was a group of them who lived in one particular area, you may be able to buy a map that shows and names all the streets in that area back in e.g. 1860. This is helpful to see where they lived and it can only complement your file. These maps are available in many bookshops and are generally not expensive (see website list).

One set of information I find particularly useful is the directories of trades and professions. These list most of the business and professional people in many towns and villages throughout the country. If you know your ancestors had a business of some type e.g. shoemaker in Worksop in 1822, then you may well find them in these directories. I have found some of my relations and even their in-laws business is in it. It is another useful way of finding out where people lived and the work they did, as well as having a copy for your file.

Many towns have schools that have been in existence for two or three hundred years. These schools kept records of pupils who attended and many of these records are now preserved in archives around the country. Should you want to trace a young ancestor in a particular town, check with the local archive office to see if they have any records of schools.

From the age of fourteen many people took an apprenticeship, which usually lasted six years. When starting the apprenticeship, they completed a contract with their employer, known as indentures, which was signed by both parties. There may be some of your ancestors who served an apprenticeship to be a blacksmith or carpenter etc. You may find it helpful to look in your local archives for details of apprenticeships to help in the compilation of your family history file.

Check the telephone directory in the area you are researching to see if there is anyone with the surname you are interested in. This is especially helpful if your ancestors came from rural communities, as they may not have moved areas for hundreds of years. You may find others with the same surname as yours. If you do, then it may be worth writing to them, sending some details of ancestors and asking if they have any information on their family history along with a S.A.E. You may find long lost relations as I have done and be able to combine your information.

I must mention the importance of sending a stamp addressed envelope if you do decide to take this line of enquiry, or when writing to anyone on family history matters. Many genealogists are very eager to share their work with you, but stop for a minute and think about the cost of the photocopies, envelope and postage, and remember to write afterwards and say 'thank you'. You may well find that if you send ten letters you may get three replies.

The Dade records (William Dade) were used mainly in Yorkshire from 1777 – 1812 as a method of recording births. These records showed three generations of a family along with the wives and their maiden names and the professions of the males and place they lived. I was lucky enough to have some of my ancestors recorded in 'Dade style' in the parish register. It makes it a lot easier to trace people when you are given three generations together.

The industrial revolution took place generally between 1760 – 1820. At this time there was a movement from the land, due to enclosures, to the cities to work in factories. It can be difficult to keep track of one's ancestors at this time. If they were farmers and owned the land, they stayed, but agricultural labourers moved to the cities where more money could be earned.

The above are only a small sample to 'wet your appetite'. Following is a list of those mentioned above and others for you to check out.

THE YEAR CHANGE

In 1751, the country was using the Julian calendar, but this was incorrect by eleven days. Using this calendar also meant that New Years Day was 25th March and the last day of the year would have been 24th March the following year. The Chesterfield Act was passed and this saw the UK adopt the Gregorian calendar from 1st January 1752. The eleven extra days were removed when the 2nd September was followed by 14th September. This corrected the calendar and the year ended on 31st December 1752. This calendar is the one we all use now and has been in operation since that time.

FURTHER PLACES/WAYS TO OBTAIN INFORMATION

Civil Registration (St. Catherine's)   Parish Records pre1837
Registers of Electors   Window Tax Lists 1696 - 1822
Hearth Tax Lists 1662 - 1689   Monumental Inscriptions
Wills   Burial Records
Old School Records   Military Records
Convict Records   Deportation Records (Australia)
Marriage Database Records   National Burial Index
Census Records 1841 to 1901   Workhouse Records
Hangings in York/Durham Prisons   Miners & Pits Records
War Graves Commission Records   Sailors Records
Waifs & strays from census records   Photographs
Dade Records 1777-1812   Poor Law Records
Directory of Trades & Professions   Adoption Records
Historical Information on Village Life   Books
Land Tax Assessments 1690-1950   Quaker Records
Bishops Transcripts   Burke's Landed Gentry
Apprentice Indenture Records   Militia Muster Records 1757 -
Poor Law Records   Poll Tax Records
Family Search   Emigration Lists
Witchcraft Records   Immigration Lists
Death Duty Registers   Birth/Deaths at Sea 1854-1891
Methodist/Jewish Records   Protestation Returns, 1642 →
War Records of Boer War, Waterloo and other battles of the 1800's
Birth, Marriages and Deaths of Britons abroad
Church windows and monuments/wall plaques in churches

There are many other records spread far and wide across the country. Many are held at The Public Records Office, but others are held by individual Family History Societies, local archive offices or companies specialising in genealogy.

DRAWING YOUR TREE

Hopefully you have now collected all the names, dates of birth, marriage or death and details of where these events took place. Write them on a large sheet of paper, e.g. a roll of lining paper. Only write them in pen if you have confirmed the details and cross-referenced an event with dates/places on a census or another certificate, otherwise write them in pencil.

Ensure that if for example there are six children in the family, that you write the names of the children from left to right on your tree starting with the oldest one first. It is good practice and helpful to all who read it to show: -

a. Date of birth and death
b. Date of baptism
c. Age of the person
d. Profession
e. Marriage date and where
f. Who they married
g. Fathers name

This information will help to make your tree a more complete one and not just one that shows the basic information only. Draw your tree separately for each branch of the family then re-draw and join the branches up at a later date when you have most of the information

When you are researching, you may see two children in the church records belonging to the same family with the same name. It was often the case that if a child died in infancy, and many did, then the next child of the same sex born to that couple was given the same name as the one who died. If you look in the death or burial record, you will probably find the death of the first child.

In the following example, abbreviations are used as shown: -

Bu = Buried   Md = Married
D   = Died   B   = Born
Bap = Baptised   C   = Circa
P.C. = Parish Church

If you find a date of birth or death cannot be ascertained then write circa or the letter **C** before the year.

A sample tree is shown: -

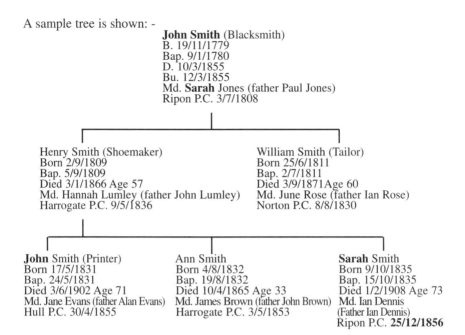

John Smith (Blacksmith)
B. 19/11/1779
Bap. 9/1/1780
D. 10/3/1855
Bu. 12/3/1855
Md. **Sarah** Jones (father Paul Jones)
Ripon P.C. 3/7/1808

Henry Smith (Shoemaker)
Born 2/9/1809
Bap. 5/9/1809
Died 3/1/1866 Age 57
Md. Hannah Lumley (father John Lumley)
Harrogate P.C. 9/5/1836

William Smith (Tailor)
Born 25/6/1811
Bap. 2/7/1811
Died 3/9/1871 Age 60
Md. June Rose (father Ian Rose)
Norton P.C. 8/8/1830

John Smith (Printer)
Born 17/5/1831
Bap. 24/5/1831
Died 3/6/1902 Age 71
Md. Jane Evans (father Alan Evans)
Hull P.C. 30/4/1855

Ann Smith
Born 4/8/1832
Bap. 19/8/1832
Died 10/4/1865 Age 33
Md. James Brown (father John Brown)
Harrogate P.C. 3/5/1853

Sarah Smith
Born 9/10/1835
Bap. 15/10/1835
Died 1/2/1908 Age 73
Md. Ian Dennis
(Father Ian Dennis)
Ripon P.C. **25/12/1856**

In the example above, notice the following: -

a. John Smith (first born) on the bottom line has the same first name as his grandfather on top line. This is following the pattern i.e. First son named after the father's father. (See section on Other Useful Information).

b. The bottom right example, Sarah Smith, was married on Christmas Day. This was popular in the 1800's to be married and/or baptised on Christmas Day.

c. The three people on the bottom line are placed on the tree in birth order.

d. The bottom right person, Sarah Smith, is named after her father's mother being the second girl in the family. (See section on Other Useful Information).

PRODUCING A FAMILY HISTORY FILE

Being able to collect all the information then draw your family tree is important, but along with it you need to assemble any birth, marriage or death certificates, photographs and other historical information you have. The file can be arranged with the tree in front and each generation going back, separated by dividers.

Within each section, which would cover a generation, there should be the relevant certificates and photographs, newspaper details etc, and a short written piece describing the village back in their time. It is useful to include any trade directory, if available, (especially if your ancestors name is on it) because it mentions the different trades that existed in their time.

As a general rule, if your ancestors lived for example in Lincoln, then you can gain a lot of information from the Lincoln archives, family history society there and other historical and genealogical places in that area. Wherever they lived is where some of your information will be held.

Other information you would probably require like the St Catherine's Index and war records are countrywide and you will obtain them from your own local archives, library, or the internet.

Copies of census returns show the family units in many cases, so include them for any years you can, along with any other newspaper cuttings or other information that may be of interest, e.g. military service details and honours, degree certificates or other items.

In the back of your file, put any other indirect information you may collect along the way like certificates or census details of brothers and sisters of your direct relations, photographs of their gravestones and computer printouts of other records you may have acquired.

Many people compile family trees but to complete it you need to add extra information as described above. You may think a map showing places of birth of ancestors is not necessary to include in your file. It is not now that it matters but in 30 or 50years time when your great grandchildren pick up your family tree file. They may be living in a different part of the country but can see at once, the place where their ancestors came from. This information and any other items you may wish to include in your file can only improve it for the benefit of others to read in future years.

When you have all the information in order and your family tree drawn and included in the file, together with the other information as described above, it is now time to write the final piece, 'A History of the _ _ _ _ _ _ Family through the Centuries'. You may like to type the sheet in old English script to give it that old world touch. This can be as short or as long as you want it to be but it should mention the following: -

a. Common names in your family that run through the generations (as I described earlier)

b. Some of the trades and professions your ancestors had.

c. A description of the areas of the country your ancestors lived in with some dates.

d. Ages some of your ancestors lived to e.g. 100 or died early e.g. 2 months.

e. A short summary of what life may have been like back in the 1600's or time you have studied.

f. Any other notable information worthy of a place on this page which when completed can be placed in the front of the book next to the tree.

Use plastic type pockets to put all your information into, this will separate, protect and keep it clean. To finish your file, a label on the front showing exactly what the file represents and the dates from and to along with the name of the person who compiled it and date compiled, will finish it off nicely.

Once you have completed your file you may want copies for your relations, sons and daughters. It is good to have at least one other copy in case the original went missing or was damaged resulting in many years of work lost.

I hope you have found the compiling of your family history as interesting and exciting as I did. It may have brought to light some interesting pieces of information and even revelations! Whatever it has done, I hope it has brought satisfaction in compiling it, and that this booklet has helped you at least to get started in Family Research.

When your family tree is finally complete and you think you have constructed a reasonable tree, send a copy to The Society of Genealogists in London (see Useful Addresses) for use in their library. It is nice to think that all your hard work, sometimes over many years, will be in their library for anyone to look at and for future generations to see.

A CHRONOLOGY OF BRITISH GENEALOGY

1349 Black death reached England.

1388 Statute of Cambridge restricted movements of labourers & beggars.

1494 Vagabond and Beggars Act

1536 Dissolution of the monasteries.

1538 Thomas Cromwell orders parishes to record baptism, marriages and burials.

1539 First Criminal Court set up at The Old Bailey.

1540 Statute of Wills. Boys could make wills from age 14 and girls from 12.

1576 Act introduced for setting the poor to work.

1588 Spanish Armada sighted off the Lizard, Cornwall.

1597 Act for the relief of the poor, churchwardens to oversee.

1598 Act requiring all parishes to send parish record transcripts to the Bishops.

1601 Act for relief of poor.

1603 Bubonic plague throughout London.

1603 Elizabeth 1 dies.

1605 Guy Fawkes discovered.

1620 Plymouth Colony at Cape Cod established by Mayflower emigrants.

1626 Press gangs start about this time.

1641 First battles between roundheads and cavaliers.

1642 English Civil War.

1643 Quakers founded by George Fox.

1643 Excise Duty introduced

1662 Settlement Act provided for relief and settlement of the poor in the parish they were born in and removal of those not from the parish.

1662 Hearth Tax introduced

1664 The Conventicle Act. Nonconformist worship in groups of more than 5 people banned.

1665 Plague kills many in London.

1666 Great Fire of London.

1680 Act brought in a registration fee (but generally ignored).

1689 Hearth Tax abolished.

1690 Battle of The Boyne.

1691 Quaker founder George Fox died.

1694 Sliding scale of registration fees set up for burials, marriages and baptisms.

1696 Window Tax introduced.

1696 'Paupers Passports' Act stated that poor people could enter a parish if they had a settlement certificate.

1701 Act of Settlement barred Catholics from the throne of England.

1703 John Wesley born.

1717 Freemasons Grand Lodge of England founded.

1723 Knatchbulls Act – workhouse test Act.

1744 British and French at war.

1745 Jacobite Rebellion.

1746 Battle of Culloden.

1750 Height of press gangs

1751-2 Chesterfield Act. - Gregorian Calendar introduced. Year corrected by 11 days and New Years Day changed from 25th March to 1st January.

1754 Lord Hardwicke's Act required all marriages to be performed in a church (except for Jews and Quakers, also banns must be called before the marriage.

1772 Slavery abolished

1774 First Unitarian church opened in London.

1778 Catholic Relief Act.

1783 Stamp duty of imposed on every entry recorded in parish register.

1783 Tyburn, London, used for last time as an execution place.

1784 Mail coach runs from Bristol to London.

1787 First convicts transported to Botany Bay.

1791 John Wesley died.

1795 Poor Law introduced.

1801 First National Census held.

1801 General Enclosure Act.

1805 Nelson died at Battle of Trafalgar.

1811 Primitive Methodists founded.

1812 Rose's Act. separate registers to be kept for baptisms, marriages and burials.

1815 Napoleon defeated at Waterloo.

1817 Potato famine kills many in Ireland.

1822 The Manchester Guardian Newspaper introduced.

1822 Window Tax abolished

1826 Press gangs diminish.

1831 Congregational church formed.

1832 Representation of the People Act.

1833 Abolition of Slavery Act.

1834 Act to unite parishes in unions administered by guardians.

1834 Poor Law Amendment Act.

1836 Marriages in dissenting chapels legalised.

1836 General Register Office established.

1837 Civil Registration (St. Catherine's) started in England, Scotland and Wales.

1838 Public Record Office established.

1840 Photography developed.

1840 Penny Post started.

1841 National Census taken.

1844 Mines Act prohibits use of women and boys in mines.

1849 Wesleyan Reform church founded.

1849 Cholera epidemic.

1851 National Census taken.

1852 Act of Parliament creates Patent Office.

1853 Abolition of convicts to Australia.
1854 Crimean War.
1856 End of Crimean War.
1857 United Methodist Free Church founded.
1857 Probate Court set up by Parliament.
1858 Country divided into civil probate districts.
1861 National Census taken.
1865 Salvation Army founded.
1868 Last public hanging in Britain.
1871 Trade Union Act legalised all trade unions.
1871 National census taken.
1876 Settlement Act repealed.
1880 Non conformist ministers given the right to perform burials in C. of E.
   churchyards.
1881 National Census taken.
1882 Church Army founded.
1882 Married Women's Property Act. Married women could not make a will
   without her husbands consent.
1883 Boys Brigade founded.
1888 Hand held camera invented.
1891 National Census taken.
1899 Start of Boer War.
1901 National Census taken.
1902 End of Boer War.
1911 National Census taken.
1912 Titanic sinks more than 1500 drowned.
1914 Britain declares war on Germany.
1918 War ends
1929 Age of Marriage Act. Prevented people under the age of 16 from marrying.
   Before that date, boys could marry at age 14 and girl's age12.
1939 Britain at war with Germany.
1945 War ends.
1972 United reformed church formed by joining Congregational Church and
   Presbyterian Church.

This list is given as a guide to help the genealogist with dates and notable events
from 1349. It is given as a genealogy list, not as a chronology of British history.
Should you wish to enquire further into any of the above items, I suggest you
search on the internet for each title, where there is a fuller explanation.

Any of the above points may have a bearing on your family tree e.g. if an ancestor
went to fight in one of the many wars through the centuries, was a passenger on
the Titanic or transported to Australia.

FAMILY HISTORY SOCIETIES

These societies are operated by the public for the public. The aims of the society are to promote the study of genealogy and family history and to educate the public by holding meetings and sharing information as well as giving assistance and producing publications. There is usually a small yearly membership fee, but all the societies hold a wealth of information local to their area. If you have ancestors who lived in another part of the country, then I recommend you join the family history society in that area, not where you live now.

Each individual branch of the FHS holds local information on things like monumental inscriptions, parish records, burial databases and local census returns often from 1841 to 1901, along with other information to help you locate your elusive ancestors.

You can get help with searches for individuals, who you may not be able to find, but which an experienced member of the society, with knowledge, can track down for you. Usually there is a small fee for this. A quarterly magazine is usually produced by each branch, which is of interest and awaited eagerly by members. You can contribute to the magazine and forward queries to the magazine.

USEFUL WEBSITES

Office of National Statistics	www.ons.gov.uk
Family Search	www.familysearch.org
Cyndi's List	www.cyndislist.com
Public Record Office	www.pro.gov.uk/genealogy
1901 Census	www.census.pro.gov.uk
Scots Origins (pay site)	www.origins.net./gro
Society of Genealogists	www.sog.org.uk
U.K.and Ireland Genealogy	www.genuki.org.uk
Old Maps	www.alangodfreymaps.co.uk
Genealogy on the internet	www.spub.co.uk/fgi/index.html
Roots Web	www.rootsweb.com
Royal Commission on Historical Manuscripts	www.hmc.gov.uk
Federation of Family History Societies	www.ffhs.org.uk
Trade Directories	www.historicaldirectories.org
Middlesbrough,Stockton & Hartlepool Indexes.	www.teesvalley-indexes.co.uk

USEFUL ADDRESSES

Federation of Family History Societies
PO Box 2425
Coventry,
CV5 6YX
Tel. 07041 492032

General Register Office,
PO Box 2,
Southport. PR8 2JD
Tel.0151 4714200

(You can send here for copies of birth, marriage and death certificates, they can be expensive but in the local register offices they cost £7.00)

Society of Genealogists,
14, Charterhouse Buildings,
Goswell Rd,
London. EC1M 7BA

(also the Guild of One Name Studies at this address c/o box G).

General Register Office for Scotland,
New Register House,
3 West Register St,
Edinburgh. EH1 3YT
Tel. 0131 3340380

(Scottish civil registration records)

Public Record Office,
Ruskin Avenue,
Kew, Richmond,
Surrey. TW9 4DU
Tel. 0208 3925200

(Contains many records going back hundreds of years covering life in Britain)

The Family Records Centre,
First Floor, Public Record Office,
1 Mydlleton St,
London.
EC1R 1UW
Tel. 0208 3925300

Census returns 1841 – 1901
(They have civil registration records also)

Commonwealth War Graves Commission,
2 Marlow Road,
Maidenhead,
Berkshire SL6 7DX
Tel. 01628 634221

1st and 2nd world war graves information also excellent web site with names of those fallen.

THE FAMILY TREE

The family tree, the family tree,
who shall we put in the family tree.
There's grandma and grandad,
they're in for a start,
and old auntie Mildred,
she too plays a part.
Then there's that uncle Silas,
a bit of a card,
we might miss him off though,
It wouldn't be hard,
and great grandad Tom,
who ran off to sea,
he's just got to be in the family tree.
One aunt never married,
but she wasn't a prude,
she still had six children
did great aunt Gertrude.
There are uncles and auntie's
and cousins galore,
and Henry's and Rachel's,
and Fred's by the score.
Just who is entitled to roost in our tree,
Oop's there's one I forgot,
I had better put <u>me.</u>

W.R.Fyfe.

Should you wish to comment on this book or give further information to help keep it updated for the benefit of others in future, please write to the address below or e:mail via our website: -

Challenge Publications
7 Earlsmere Drive
Ardsley
Barnsley
S71 5HH
www.chall-pub.fsnet.co.uk

NOTES

NOTES